GW01424325

Teach Yourself
KARATE

Kunal Nagi

SPORTS PUBLICATION

G-6, 23/23-B, EMCA House, Ansari Road,
Darya Ganj, New Delhi-110002
Ph.: (O) 65749511 (M) 9868028838
(R) 27562163   Telefax: 011-23240261
E-mail: lakshaythani@hotmail.com

Published by:

SPORTS PUBLICATION
G-6, 23/23-B, EMCA House, Ansari Road, Darya Ganj, New Delhi-2
Ph. : (O) 65749511 (R) 27562163, (Telefax) 23240261 (M) 9868028838
E-mail: *lakshaythani@hotmail.com*

© 2007 Publishers

I.S.B.N. – 978-81-7879-458-7

PRINTED IN INDIA 2007

All Rights Reserved

No part of this publication may be stored in a retrieval system, transmitted, or reproduced in any way, including but not limited to photocopy, photograph, magnetic or other record, without the prior agreement and written permission of the publisher.

Laser Typeset by:
JAIN MEDIA GRAPHICS,
C-4/95-A, Keshav Puram, (Near Subhash Place), Delhi-110035
Phones: 011-20296366, 9911151534, 9350556511

Printed by:
CHAWLA OFFSET PRINTERS
Delhi-110052

Price: Rs. 95/-

CONTENTS

PREFACE

Teach Yourself Karate provides methods of teaching and spotting beginning Karate skills. Emphasis are placed on giving the teacher a guide for working with a typical physical education class and providing a basis to individuals having the ability to excel in the sport.

Teachers should encourage students to attain success without being totally concerned with perfect performance. The Skills covers all the tactics, techniques of Karate.

The whole book is designed into 3 chapters:

The First chapter consists of information regarding the ancient history and development of Karate.

The Second Chapter explains the difference between Karate and Judo.

The concluding chapter exhibits all the essential Skills and Techniques of Karate with illustrations where necessary.

Hopefully, the present study will prove very useful for the sportsperson, teachers, students of physical education as well as for the general readers.

—Publisher

1

HISTORICAL BACKGROUND OF KARATE

The word karate itself literally means empty-hand. It is pronounced as kah-rah-teh. Although the early origins of the art are traced to China, it owes its development to the inhabitants of the Luchu Islands which are situated approximately 200 miles to the south-west of Japan. The name Luchu is pronounced Ryukyu by the Japanese.

Karate is an unusual activity in that even its exponents are unable to agree fully upon its aims. Self-defence, martial art or sport. Karate is a series of self-defence movements and counter-attacks based on traditional Karate. These are run into a formal series, called Katas, which are taught and practised until a high standard of proficiency is reached. There are several styles and each style retains its own Katas which seldom, if ever, change.

At the beginning of the seventieth century the islands were conquered by the Japanese under the Daimyo of Satsuma. The Luchuans continued to pay tribute to both China and Japan till 1879 when the king was brought captive to Tokyo and the government was reorganized as a Japanese prefecture under the style of Okinawa Ken, as it has since been called. Like their Chinese predecessors the Japanese conquerors would not allow the natives to carry weapons of any kind. But for their self-protection against their alien oppressors the natives cleverly circumvented this ukase by devising and elaborating the system of bare-hand fighting now known as karate.

It was Okinawa karate master Funakoshi who introduced it into Japan proper as karate-do, or the way of karate. In this altered name, we can detect an analogy with judo in which the word 'do' meaning way was substituted by the late Dr. Jigoro Kano, the founder of the judo, to emphasize the ethical basis of his new eclectic system of self-defence.

Thus the present day protagonists of karate are equally insistent on the purpose of their art as a means not of aggression but of self-defence over and above its alleged value as a system of physical culture par excellence, and although not denying the ability of trained karateka to smash boards, pulverize tiles and bricks and pierce bamboo fences with their hardened bare hands and finger-tips, they deprecate unilateral absorption in the purely physical attributes of karate to the exclusion of its alleged spiritual rationale.

It is even contended that certain movements of the karate katas or forms are specially designed to purify the performers' spirit and are therefore congruent with the maxim Karate ni sente nashi, which can be freely interpreted to mean that there is no first attack in karate.

Evidence of the desire of karate's responsible leadership to discourage the prominence currently given to the physical manifestations of the art can be discerned in Reikichi Oya's timely reminder that there is a considerable difference between a static wooden board, a heap of tiles or bricks, and a living moving, perhaps armed opponent bent upon putting paid to one's earthly account at close quarters.

Judo is called the way of gentleness, whereas karate is often dubbed the power way. In karate, the full power of the body is invoked when a blow is dealt, but this fact represents only one facet of the truth. It would be incomplete did it leave out of account the many occasions when small but well-trained karateka have defeated opponents veterans have easily disposed of powerful but inexperienced youngsters. Although many of the amazing stories recounted about past karate masters may be dismissed as apocryphal, the authenticity of modern version can be vouched for.

Karate kata differ from those of judo or sumo in that the performer can at his discretion suitably regulate the degree of strength needed for their execution. Thus the physically powerful performer can give an exhibition replete with force while the weak performer can adapt his display to his individual capacity and execute the kata lightly. Or again the strong man is at liberty to infuse an optional amount of strength into his demonstration in accordance with the daily condition of his body.

In this manner, the limitation of sex are taken into consideration and even when he or she suffers from certain physical disabilities he or she can easily practise karate. Then again, seeing that there are as many as thirty different kinds of kata in present-day karate, the performer can at any time choose those to his liking and freely execute a given number.

TEACH YOURSELF KARATE

You need not spend a lot of money for practising the event as no special premises or equipments are required for the practice of karate. If a mat-covered floor is not available, an ordinary boarded floor will do equally well, or an open space of ground will suffice for the execution of the karate kata.

2

KARATE—DIFFERENT FROM JUDO

It is extremely difficult to define Karate. It is linked in the public mind with Judo but no doubt this is because both developed in Japan and both are practised in similar garments. In fact the Karate jacket, not having to take much strain from pulling and tugging, is much lighter in weight but this is not obvious on a casual inspection. In both, participants work in bare feet. Not so long ago Judo men, on attaining the distinction of black belt, were introduced to atemi which is the art of disabling opponents by striking at nerve centres and other vital part of the body. Karate is a further development of this form of fighting.

It is said that Karate developed when the Japanese, having overrun the Luchu Islands, refused to allow the Islanders to carry weapons. As a result Karate was devised as the only form of self-defence available to them.

Like Judo, the word 'do' meaning way was added. This was intended to indicate that Karate-do had an ethical basis and was not just a form of aggression or self-defence. The present-day Karate men insist that whilst their art is a most effective form of self-defence, this is only in addition to its value as a form of physical and mental training.

Karate, like Judo, has developed a philosophy of its own. There is no doubt that a trained Karateman can smash boards, tiles and bricks with his bare hands, elbows, feet and head but this is a side many experts prefer to hide away from publicity. Karate is taught in the form of a series of katas. These are series of formal exercises in which the basic movements are practised.

5

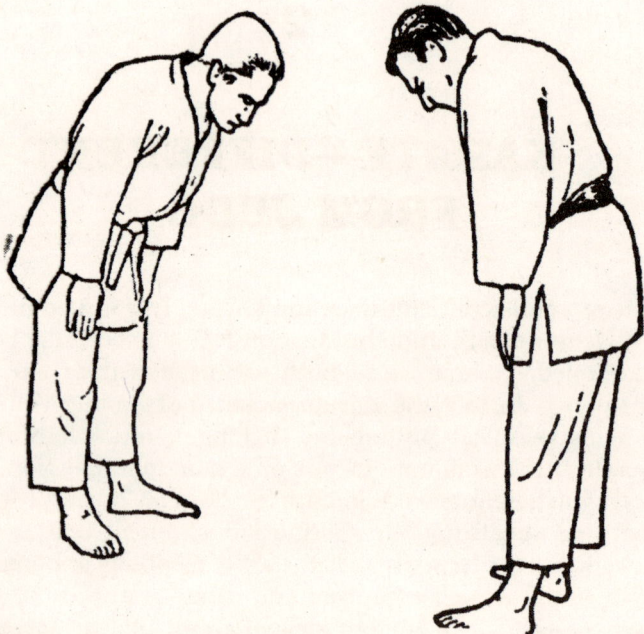

As a form of defence, Karate has several advantages over other methods. Anyone of any age can practice it and practice it alone and no special equipment is required. With reasonable precautions there is no danger, and finally no great exertion is required. Whilst reasonable proficiency can be attained from written instruction, to attain a really high standard, it is necessary to obtain expert instruction.

Meaning of karate is empty hand and all attacks are made with no more than the weapons provided by nature. These are the hand, foot, elbow, head and knees. It is important to use these weapons correctly as failure to do so will not only reduce the effect of the blow but may cause painful injury to the Karateman.

3

SKILLS AND TECHNIQUES OF KARATE

It is told earlier that no equipment or apparatus is being used in Karate. Parts of body are used as equipments by the performer. Thus, the basic thing to learn in karate is to make proper use of various parts of bodies.

Basic Posture

In the basic posture, the body of the performer should be upright with his feet placed about shoulder-width apart. His arms hang relaxed with his hands lightly clenched in front of him, one either side of the knot of his belt.

Alternate Basic Posture

There is a second Basic Posture which is used when protecting the upper part of the body and making counter-attacks on the upper part of the attacker's body.

In this case the arms are bent at the elbows, the fists being held level with the shoulders, palms of the hands facing the shoulders. Having warded off a blow to the head with, say the left arm, there is no need to take the fist back to the basic position at the hip. Instead it can be taken back to the shoulder.

Attack A

Step I—From the basic posture the left leg and arm are advanced, the right hand being taken back and down to the right hip. A left-hand blow is delivered and the right hand and arm take up the defensive role.

Step II—The right leg and arm are moved forward, the left hand moving back to the hip. The movement must be dynamic, both arms and leg moving at the same speed, the leg reaching the ground shortly before the arm reaches the conclusion of its movement as it has far less to travel.

You can repeat these steps as many times as your stamina and the time available will allow. Repeated punches will however, tend to stretch the muscles and joints of the arms with the result that you can develop a painful elbow. Because of this, you should perform this with a lot of care and at short sessions in the beginning.

Attack B

Step I—From the Basic Posture advance your left foot and arm, at the same time taking your right arm back a little. This position is the sort of defensive posture you would expect to adopt again an attack with the right leg or hand. Your left, defensive arm is held forward, the arm almost parallel with the left thigh but about 18 to 247 inches above it, as convenient and comfortable.

The left side of the body is now facing the imaginary opponent, with the eyes watching his face. The left hand is lightly clenched. Your right arm is bent at the elbow at a little more than 90 degree with the hand open or lightly clenched, ready to attack. The posture is strong and well balanced.

As in a Judo attack, the hips have been lowered by bending the knees, in this case the left, and the lower abdomen has been made strong. Resume the Basic Posture.

Step II—Your right foot and leg are advanced, the left fist being taken back against the left hip. This is a fast dynamic movement, the leg and both arms moving at the same speed. Should your left arm move more slowly than the right you will lose balance, and in addition, should the opponent evade your blow, you will be weak defensively.

On the other hand, should the right hand move slowly, there will be insufficient power to your attack. The right foot is advanced along the ground in a gliding movement. Raising the leg in this condition results in the arc of the blow of your fist being deflected and wakened. Do not overstride with your leg as this will again weaken the blow and cause you to loose balance.

The right forearm is turned so that the back of the hand is upwards. The wrist is absolutely straight and the fist, wrist, forearm, and upper-arm are in a straight line from your shoulder. The blow is aimed at the chest or middle of the opponent's body. The left fist is placed at your hip, loosely clenched, where it is ready to deal with any counter-attack by warding-off or catching a blow.

It is important that the shoulders should be kept down. To raise the shoulders, as if shrugging them, weakens the posture and greatly reduces the effect of the blow. The trunk is again kept upright, the eyes looking into the eyes of your opponent.

Attack C

Step I—From the basic posture, advance your left leg and arm, the right fist coming down to the right hip. Your left arm thrusts downwards and to your front to catch the opponent's right arm or leg as he attacks your body.

In this Karate movement, it is the custom to catch the opponent's shin or forearm and push it downwards, but having been brought up in Judo, however, this is quite inefficient and dangerous to the fingers and thumbs. Instead, ward-off the attack with the fist or an outward chopping movement of the little finger edge of the forearm is much recommended.

This movement allows more room for possible misjudgment and can, if well directed, disable the opponent's arm or leg.

Step II—As the attack is turned away, take the right leg and arm forward, driving your fist downward to your opponent's solar-plexus, abdomen or groin as convenient.

Attack D

Step I—This defence is originated by stepping to your rear, and is called a rear-step defence.

From the basic posture, you take your right leg back, driving the left fist forward at the same time. Your right fist comes down to your right hip. This first movement is likely to be that used to block an opponent's blow.

Attack E

Step I—Made from the basic posture, but instead of attacking the middle of the opponent's body, this time your blow is aimed at his face. The blow should be aimed at targets such as his forehead, eyes or the vital spot beneath his note. You might use the fingers or the fist with one or two knuckles advanced to make contact.

From the basic position, advance your left foot and arm, moving the arm so that the blow is aimed at the opponent's face. The right hand comes down to the right hip.

Step II—The right fist and leg drive forward, the left fist coming back to the left hip. As in all the movements, the attacking arm is held so that the back of the hand is upward, the wrist and forearm being completely straight. The head is upright and the trunk kept straight.

You can either start from the basic posture by taking the step to the rear or alternately make a third step punching forward with the left fist and so on.

Attack F

The attacker aims his attack at the upper part of your body. That is to say his target is your shoulders, neck or head.

Step I—From the Basic Posture, step back with your right foot, sweeping your left arm, fist clenched, upwards and outwards to ward-off the attack. The right fist is placed by your right hip. The ward-off is made with the little finger side of the fist and forearm.

Step II—Step forward with your right leg, driving your right fist upwards and forwards. The target for your counter is your opponent's head, face or throat.

As you drive forward with your right fist, your left is brought back to your left hip at exactly the same speed.

Attack G

This is a complicated movement to describe, requiring as it does the use of both arms in quick succession. It is a ward-off and counter-attack with the little finger cutting edges of the hands. The opponent attacks with fist or foot to your body at about stomach level.

Step I—From the Basic Posture, you take back your right foot, your right arm being raised across your chest and your left held in front of you. Both arms are bent at the elbow with the hands so turned that the little finger edges are pointed downwards. In effect, the arms are bent in much the same way as a whip is coiled ready to strike.

Step II—You make a sweeping drive downwards and outwards with your left hand thrusting away an attack. The little finger edge of the left hand and the forearm is used to ward-off, the hard bony side contacting the soft inside of the attacker's right leg or arm.

Step III—Step forward with the right foot, at the same time whipping the right forearm down and outwards to deliver a cripping counter-blow. The counter is aimed at one of the vital points.

Attack H

Here we will discuss kicks. It must be remembered that kicks can be warded-off or the leg caught, so it is essential that the Karateman delivers his kick at lightening speed without sacrificing his balance. The foot must be withdrawn fast whether or not the kick has landed.

Step I—Adopt the basic posture with your fists close to your hips, one on either side of the knot of your belt. Now glide forward with the left leg.

Step II—Keeping your fists at your hips, kick forward and upwards with your right leg. The contact with the opponent is made with the ball of the foot. As you kick, the left knee is bent to improve your balance and although you kick as far forward and upward as you can, you must keep your trunk upright to preserve your balance.

To conclude the movement, bring the foot down and resume the basic posture. Do not raise on the ball of the foot upon which you are standing or this may cause you to fall backwards. Now kick with the other foot.

Attack I

This attack is delivered with the big toe edge of the foot. Because this movement involves crossing the feet, which is a basic error, and kick has not very much range, it is not considered to be a very effective attack.

Step I—From the basic posture, balance on your left leg, bending the knees slightly, and kick across your left leg at an opponent at your left side. The kick is aimed at his knee or shin. Your fists are kept at your hips and your trunk upright.

Step II—Repeat the kick to your right with your left foot.

Attack J

This is a kick to the side that is to your right or left delivered with the little toe edge of the foot.

Step I—From the Basic Posture, bend your left knee slightly for balance and kick outwards to the right with the right foot. The right leg is kept straight, the inside edge of the foot being aimed at the opponent's knee or shin. Always kick as high as you possibly can, but your trunk must be kept upright and your fists at your hips.

Step II—Repeat the kick, this time using the left foot.

Attack K

Step I—From the basic posture, step forward with your right foot, punching at the opponent's face with your right fist. The left hand remains at the left hip. The trunk is kept upright and the right shoulder not advanced. Take the right foot and leg back, returning to the basic posture.

Attack L

Step I—Adopt the basic posture. Take a longish gliding step forward with the right foot, at the same time punching forward with the right fist. The left fist remains at the left hips.

This is a very basic movement. The blow is aimed at the opponent's chest. The trunk is kept upright and the right shoulder is not thrust forward as you punch. Return to basic posture by withdrawing the right foot.

Step II—Step forward with the left foot, punching with the left fist. The right fist being taken to the right hip. Take the left foot and leg back to regain the Basic Posture.

Attack M

Step I—Advance the left leg and punch with the right fist to the opponent's face. The left fist is taken to the left hip. As usual the trunk is kept upright and faces the front, the shoulder not being advanced as the punch is delivered. Step back and lower the fists to return to the Basic Posture.

Step II—Step forward with the right leg punching to the opponent's face with the left fist. Step back to return to the basic posture.

Attack N

This is a defence and counter to a punch delivered to your chest. It commences from the basic posture.

Step I—As the opponent punches with his right hand, step back with your right foot leaving the right fist at your hip and taking your left fist up to your right shoulder sweep outwards and upwards with your left fist and forearm. Contact is made with the little finger edge so that the palm of the hand is held downwards.

Step II—Without moving your feet, take your left fist back to your left hip at the same time, drive your right fist to the opponent's stomach or chest. Take your left leg back to resume the basic posture.

Step III—Step back with your left foot taking your right fist to your left shoulder and then sweeping outwards and upwards with it to ward-off a punch with an opponent's left fist. Your left fist remains at your hip.

Step IV—Returning your right fist to your hip, drive forward with your left fist at the same time aiming at the opponent's chest or stomach. Take your right leg back to recover the basic posture.

Attack O

This is an opposition movement in which the right arm and left leg move together as you attack.

Step I—From the basic posture, move your left foot forward leaving the left fist at the hip and at the same time punching with the right fist to the opponent's chest. The trunk is kept upright and the right shoulder not advanced. Take back the left foot and bring down your right arm to regain the basic posture.

Step II—Advance the right foot punching at the opponent's chest with the left fist. The right fist goes to your right hip. Withdraw the right leg and left fist to resume the basic posture.

Attack P

This is a defence followed by a finger thrust as the counter. Your opponent punches at your chest or face with his right hand.

Step I—Step back with your right foot and take your left fist to your right shoulder, from there sweeping outwards and upwards to ward-off the attack with the little finger edge of the hand and forearm.

Step II—Without moving your feet take your left hand back to your hip at the same time thrusting with your fingertip to the opponent's throat or other suitable vulnerable point with your right hand. Step back to the basic posture.

Step III—Step back with your left foot and taking your right fist across to your left shoulder ward-off outwards and up-wards with a straight hand, little finger edge leading.

Step IV—Returning your right fist to your hip drive, your left fingertip to your opponent's throat or other vulnerable point within reach. Step back with your right leg to regain the basic posture.

Attack Q

This is a defence against a right-hand blow aimed downward at your head.

Step I—Taking your right foot back, sweep your left fist upwards so that the fist is at least slightly higher than your head. The opponent's right hand blow is swept away with the little finger edge of your forearm. The trunk is kept upright. Your right fist is retained at the hip.

Step II—Keeping   r feet in the same position, bring your left fist down to your left hip at the same time driving your right fist into the stomach of the opponent. Return to the basic posture.

Attack R

This is a combined ward-off and counter-blow.

15

<u>Step I</u>—From the basic posture, step back with your right foot and taking your left fist up to your right shoulder sweep downwards and outwards across your body in order to dash away a kick or punch aimed at your stomach or groin. Contact is made with the little finger edge of your fist and forearm. This ward-off is a form of hammer-fist blow or a chop with the edge of the hand to the opponent's leg or arm.

<u>Step II</u>—Without moving your feet withdraw your left fist to your hip and punch with your right arm to your opponent's chest or stomach. Bring your left leg back to regain the basic posture.

<u>Step III</u>—Step forward with your right foot taking your right fist to your left shoulder and then sweeping outwards and downwards to ward-off an attack using the little finger edge of your right forearm and fist.

<u>Step IV</u>—Taking your right fist back to your right hip, punch with your left fist at your opponent's chest or stomach without moving your feet. Finally, step back with your right foot to regain the basic posture.

Attack S

In this attack, you ward-off a right-handed attack to your eyes.

<u>Step I</u>—Take back your right foot leaving your right fist at your right hip. Your left arm sweeps upwards, little finger edge leading, warding-off the thrust to your eyes. The fingers of your left hand are outstreched to add length to your defence or you can use a hammer-fist blow.

<u>Step II</u>—Without moving your feet, bring your left fist back to your left hip at the same time drive your right fist upwards to your opponent's chest or face. Withdraw your left foot and bring your fists to the hip position to resume the basic posture.

Step III—To ward-off a left-handed blow to the eyes, take back your left foot sweeping your right arm up and outwards, making contact with the little finger edge. Your left hand is retained close to the hip.

Step IV—Take your right hand back to your hip at the same time punching upwards with your left fist to the opponent's chest or face. Withdraw your right foot and bring your left fist down to resume the basic posture.

Attack T

Defence and counter to a left-handed blow to the stomach.

Step I—Take back your left foot raising the right fist over to shoulder level in front of you. The left fist is held at the hip.

Step II—Sweep the right fist downwards and outwards driving a blow to your stomach away from you.

Step III—Drive the left fist to the opponent's stomach, taking the right back to the hip. Resume the basic posture.

Attack U

Defence and counter to a right-handed blow to the stomach.

Step I—Take your right foot back keeping your right fist at the hip at the same time raising your left fist upward and forward. The little finger edge of the hand is upwards.

Step II—From this position, your left fist is swept downwards and outwards thus warding-off a blow to your stomach.

Step III—The right fist is driven to the opponent's stomach, the left being taken to the left hip. The feet are not moved. Return to the basic posture.

Ways of Planting the Feet or Ashi-no-Tachi-Kata

In the kata or forms of karate, three basic kinds are specified, i.e., musubitachi or linked posture, heisokutachi or blocked foot posture, and hachijitachi or figure of eight posture. These are in turn sub-divided into the soto-hgachijitachi or outer figure of eight posture and the uchi-hachijatchi or inner figure of eight posture.

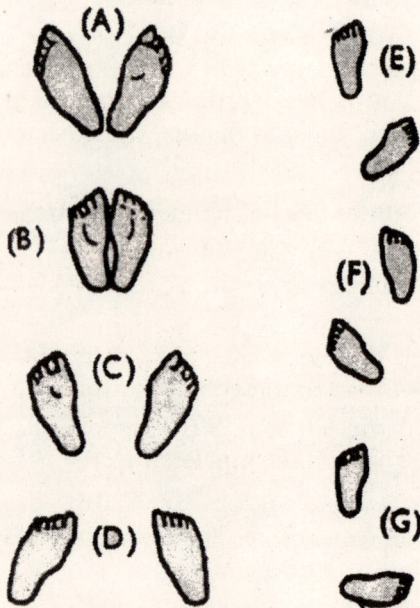

a. <u>Hachijitachi or figure of eight posture</u> : When standing in the soto-hachijitachi or outer figure of eight posture, the tips of your toes should be widely opened and in the uchi-hachijitachi or inner figure of the eight posture, your heels should widely spread.

The space between both heels depends upon the individual but generally it coincides with the space between the shoulders, say about one foot five inches. This position of foot is shown by fig. 2(i).

b. <u>Musubitachi or linked feet</u> : The left and right heels are joined with the tips of the toes turned upwards. This is a pose reminiscent of gymnastics, but strength is not infused into the shoulders and both arms are allowed to hang naturally against the sides and the eyes gaze to the front. Fig. 2(ii) shows this position of foot.

c. <u>Heisokutachi or blocked foot posture</u> : In this pose, the feet are drawn together up to the tips of the toes. This posture is shown by fig. 2(iii).

d. <u>Zenkutsutachi or inclined posture</u> : In this position, the space between your feet should differ according to your height but generally speaking, it is about 2 feet 5 inches.

The advanced right leg is bent so that from the knee to the heel, it is almost perpendicular. The rear left leg is extended and the weight of the body is evenly distributed on both legs.

e. <u>TEI Letter Posture</u> : The position of the feet resembles the Japanese ideograph T; hence, its name.

f. <u>RE Letter Posture</u> : There are two positions, viz., left and right.

g. <u>Neko-Ashitachi or cat foot posture</u> : Here your weight should rest on your rear bent leg while your front leg also bent but with the heel raised from the ground and the toes lightly applied to it. This posture is regarded as suitable for advance performers.

h. Kokutsutachi or retroflex posture : This is a posture the reverse of the zentuksutachi. This, in this case, your rare left leg should be bent so that from the knee to the heel, it is approximately perpendicular. Your forward right leg is outstretched. The weight of your body rests on your rare leg and the space between both feet is about 2 feet 5 inches.

i. Kibatachi or Equestrian Posture : In the somewhat cryptic karate terminology, this posture is also called the

naifu-anchi-tachi or anti-knife posture. The toes of both your feet are turned slightly inwards with the heels opened more than the toes.

Strength is infused into the inner sides of the thighs. Both knees are adequately bent so that from the knees downwards the leg is almost perpendicular. Again strength is infused into the outer edge of the soles of both feet. Your upper body is held upright, both shoulders lowered, the chest extended, the hips dropped and power infused into the lower abdomen familiar to all judo students under

20

its Japanese name of saika tanden.

j. Shikotachi or Four Thigh Posture : In this posture, your toes and knee-caps are turned outwards, i.e., as in the outer figure of eight posture; both your legs are widely opened, both knees bent, the upper body held upright and the hips dropped.

k. Sagi-Ashitachi or Heron Leg Posture : In this position, one foot is lifted about as high as your other knee. If the lifted leg comes in front of the knee, the posture is called mae-sagi-ashitachi or front heron leg posture; if behind, the ushiro-sagi-ashitachi or rear heron leg posture.

l. Fudotachi or Immobile Posture : In this posture, your legs are a little more widely opened than in the zenkutsutachi. Both knees are adequately bent and both legs on an average equally share the weight of the body. The toes of both right and left foot point in the same direction.

m. Sansentachi or Three Battle Posture : Emanating from the kibatachi and in that style, you stand so that either the left or right foot is brought forward the distance from the toes to the heel.

Leg and Foot Technique or Ashiwaza

The roots of the toes at the bottom of a raised foot when the toes are curved are likened to a pigeon's chest. They should be the equivalent of the normal fist and constitute the basis of keriwaza or kicking techniques.

When the foot is being used to kick forward with the toes adequately curved, if strength is not infused into the ankle, there is risk of injury so that care in this respect should always be taken.

a. Ushirokakato or Back Heel : This is used for the ushirogeri or rear kick. When, for example, your waist is

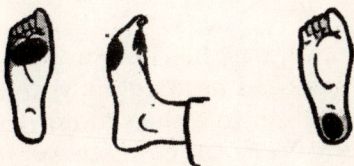

encircled from behind or your hand is twisted in the reverse direction the rear kick can be effectively used against your opponent's scrotum or shin.

b. <u>Bottom of Foot</u> : Parts of the heel on the under surface

of the foot. It performs a very useful supplementary function when, for example, you tread powerfully down upon your opponent's instep, when delivering the keriage or upward kick, the kerihanashi or kick release.

c. <u>Ashizoko or Foot Bottom</u> : With the so-called flat of the foot, you sweep away the opponent's foot or ward off his thrusting fist.

d. <u>Ashikuri or Ankle</u> : Your toes are stretched in a straight line with your shin in which position with the ankle you kick your opponent's scrotum.

e. <u>Ashigatana or Footsword</u> : As in the case of the bottom of the raised foot, you curve the toes upward and use the little-toe edge of the foot for the fumikomi or step-in, the kerihanashi or kick release, the yokogeri or lateral kick, to attack your opponent's knee joints, flank.

Care must be taken not to apply the root of the little toe. The ashigatana corresponds to the tegatana among the hand techniques.

After the opponent's attack has been warded-off with the arm cr the arm has been used not only to ward-off, but also to pull the attacker into the counter-blow, you can use your foot and knee as counter-weapons. Below different kinds in which an opponent can attack is mentioned alongwith the ways in which you have to tackle his attack.

Attack A

The opponent, with his right arm, aims a blow to your head or upper body.

Step I—The blow is warded-off with an upward and outward sweep of the left arm, fingers extended. At the same time, you step forward with your left foot. As the blow is warded-off, bring the right knee up into the attacker's middle body or left side should he have turned.

Step II—The blow is again warded-off as you step forward with the left foot with an upwards and outwards sweep of the left arm, fingers extended.

As you ward-off the blow, turn the wrist clockwise and grip the inside of the attacker's right sleeve, pulling him in the direction of his blow. This will turn him so that his front is towards you. Counter with an upward drive of your right knee to the middle of his body.

Step III—Ward-off the blow with an outward and upward sweep of the left hand, drawing the attacker in the direction of his blow by a pull on his sleeve. Now bring the left knee up into his middle body or right side.

Step IV—The attacker again uses his right arm to your head or upper body but this time, you ward-off the blow with an upward and outward sweep of your right arm. To do this, the right fist is taken from the basic posture to the left hip before the sweep commences.

As the blow is deflected the attacker tends to turn his

back on you so that the left knee can be driven into the base of his spine or his back.

Attack B

The opponent attacks with a left-foot kick to your middle body from the front.

Step I—As the left foot kick is delivered, ward-away his leg with a downward and outward sweep of your left arm, stepping in with your left leg. Counter with an upward drive of your right knee to the base of his spine.

Step II—Ward-off the left-foot, kick to your middle body with a downward and outward sweep of the left arm, but do not step in with the left foot.

As there is now a reasonable distance between you and your opponent, counter by kicking to his left side with your right foot.

Step III—Deflect the left-footed kick to your body by sweeping outward and downward with your right arm, stepping in with your right foot as you do so. As this ward-off pushes his left leg outward, drive your left knee upwards into his groin.

Attack C

This is the counter to a left-handed blow to the head or upper body.

Step I—Ward-off the blow with an upward and outward sweep of the right hand and arm, keeping the fingers straight and stepping forward with the right foot as you do so. Immediately, bring up the left knee into the opponent's middle body, or right side should he have turned, as his blow was deflected.

Step II—Deflect the left-handed blow with an upwards and outwards sweep of the right arm, stepping in with the right foot. The fingers are extended.

As you ward-off the blow, turn the hand and wrist anti-clockwise to grip the inside of the sleeve or arm and draw him forward in the direction of his blow. Counter by driving your left knee upwards into the front of his body.

Step III—Ward-off the blow as in second step, but this time counter by driving the right knee up into the attacker's middle body or left side.

Step IV—Ward-off the left-handed blow to the head by taking the left fist from the basic posture, at the right hip across to the left hip and then sweeping upwards and across your body. This deflects the blow past your left shoulder.

Step forward with the left foot as the warding-off action is made. Counter with an upward drive of the right knee to the base of the spine or back.

Attack D

These are counters to the face against an opponent who has attacked from your front and who, after his attack has been deflected, is close to you.

Step I—The attacker punches to your head or upper body with his right fist. Step in with the left foot, deflecting the blow with an outward and upward sweep of your left arm. As you do so, bring your right arm round his head from the outside, pull down his head and counter by driving your right knee upward into his face.

Step II—The attack is a left-handed punch to your head or upper body. Step in with the right foot, warding-off the blow with an outward and upward sweep of your right arm.

As you do so, take your left arm round the opponent's neck from the outside pulling his head down so that you can counter with an upward drive of your left knee to his face.

Step III—You are attacked with a right-footed kick to the middle body from your front. Step in with your left foot sweeping away the kick with an outward and downward sweep of your left arm. As you do so, your right arm round his neck from the outside and pull his head down sufficiently to enable you to counter by driving your right knee up into his face.

Step IV—To counter a left-footed kick to your middle body from the front, step forward with your right foot, warding-off the blow with a downward and outward sweep of the right arm. As the leg is warded-away, take your left arm round your opponent's neck from the outside and pull his head downward. Counter-attack by driving your left knee upwards into his face.

Step V—This attack is a downward blow to the top of your head, probably with a stick. The attack is made with the right arm.

Deflect the blow past your left shoulder with an upward and outward sweep of your left arm, stepping in as you do so with your left foot. Do not stop the downward travel of the arm but with an anti-clockwise twist of your wrist, grip the sleeve and pull the arm downward in the direction of the blow. The attacker is now bent forward.

Increase this by putting your right hand on his head and pulling forward and down. Counter by driving the right knee upwards into his face.

Step VI—You are attacked with a downward blow to the head with the left hand. The opponent would no doubt be armed with a stick to make such an attack. Deflect the blow past your right shoulder with an outward and upward sweep of your right arm, stepping in with your right foot as you do so.

By turning your right wrist clockwise, catch his arm and draw it down in the direction of his blow, thus curving the opponent's body forward. Increase the curve by placing your left hand on the top of his head or behind it and pull his head forward and downward. Counter-attack by driving your left knee upwards into the attacker's face.

Attack E

These movements are defences to kicks.

Step I—The opponent kicks to your middle body with his right foot. As he does so, ward-off the kick with a downward and outward sweep of your right arm, fingers extended, stepping in with your right foot as you do so. This leaves the opponent standing on his left foot with his right leg stretched forward at hip-level or higher. Counter by driving the left knee into the base of the opponent's spine.

Step II—This is exactly the same defensive action to a right-foot kick to your middle body described in Step I, but do not step in with the right foot. This time, the counter is a left-foot kick to the side of the opponent's body. This can only be done if there is sufficient space between you and the attacker. It is to provide this space that you do not step in.

Step III—Again the right-footed kick to your middle body. This time step in with the left foot and ward-away the attack with an outward and downward sweep with the left arm. This takes the opponent's right leg outward and upward. Immediately, counter with an upward drive of the right knee to the groin, which is fully exposed by your deflection of the kick.

Hand Technique or Tewaza

The fist is called the soul of the art. Special attention must therefore be devoted to the tempering or hardening of the fist in order to enhance the efficacy of the blows dealt with it, held in various ways.

a. Seiken or Normal Fist : There are two methods. You can keep your hands stretched with the thumb held outside. The four finger-tip as far as their roots are joined together in such wise that the first and second joints form as it were a plane, or hand can be held with the thumb slightly raised and all four finger-tips pressed into the palm. You can hold the thumb lower with the four fingers bent or thumb bent over the first finger and all four fingers pressed into the palm.

The part used for attack with the seiken or normal fist comprises the roots of the forefinger and middle finger. So much for the moment for the normal fist.

i. <u>Kentsui or Hammer Fist</u> : In this position, the lower part of the edge of the palm is used for attack and symbolizes the so-called hammer fist. While beating off the opponent's wrist the head of the fist and hard part of the joints can be used for attack.

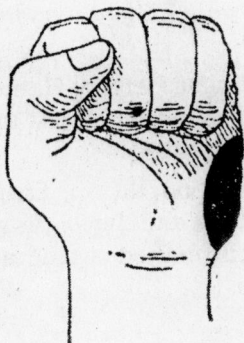

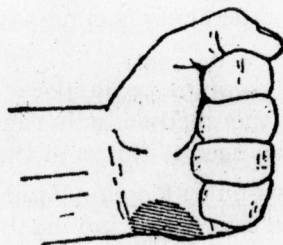

ii. <u>Hiraken, Flat or Level Fist</u> : In this method, the four fingers are arranged shallowly clasped. The thumb tip presses against the side of the forefinger. The part used for attack comprises the second joints of the forefinger and middle finger. The target of attack is the opponent's face.

iii. <u>Nakayubi-Ipponken or Middle Finger Fist</u> : With the fist held in the normal fist style, the middle finger knuckle is projected. This method is used to attack the opponent's solar-plexus and jinchu.

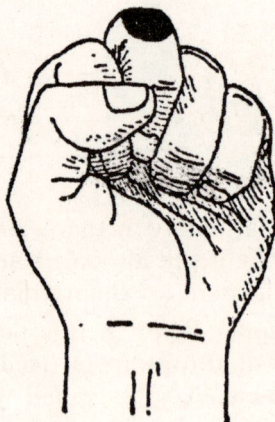

iv. <u>Uraken or Back Fist</u> : In this position, the root of the middle finger is generally used to attack the opponent's face.

v. <u>Tegatana or Handsword</u> : One Finger Piercing Hand— In this method, only the forefinger is stretched out and also used to thrust at the opponent's eyes.

<u>Two-finger Piercing Hand</u>—In this method, the ring finger, the little finger and the thumb are bent and the forefinger and the middle finger extended. This method is generally used to attack the opponent's eyes.

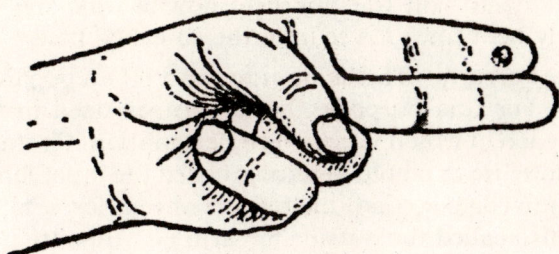

Four-Finger Piercing Hand—In this method, the thumb is bent while the other four fingers are adjusted evenly and extended. The four finger-tips are used to thrust into the opponent's solar-plexus, his sides etc.

In the same connection, we get the tate-nukite or lengthwise piercing hand in which the back of the hand is turned sideways, the fingers aligned lengthwise and used in this shape, and the hira-nukite or level piercing hand with the back of the hand turned upwards and the fingers held sideways.

Base of Palm—The palm is opened, the first joint of the thumb bent and attached to the surface of the palm. In this position, the base of the palm is used to attack the opponent's face, his shoulders, chest, with an upraised thrusting movement.

Tegatana or Handsword—In this method, the thumb is bent and the four fingers are extended. About two-thirds of the base of the palms are used in much the same way as the hammer fist.

In this manner, the handsword can be used to attack the opponent's carotid arteries, his arms, temples, middle of forehead, the jinchu, etc. But in that case, you must be careful not to let the root of the little finger be applied to the objective.

Yumi-Kobushi or Bow Fist—The thumb and forefingers are extended with the tips held downwards, the wrist strongly bent upwards to form the so-called bow.

Kote or Forearm—This is used to ward off an opponent's attack. For this purpose, the forearm is used in three ways, each of which has its own designation. First is the outer forearm or omote-kote, also called the inner forearm or thumb edge; second, the reverse or rear forearm, ura-kote, also called the outside forearm i.e., the little finger edge, and third, the level forearm, hira-kote, or centre of the outer and inner forearm, otherwise the back of the outer and reverse forearms.

Hira-Hasami—The middle finger, ring finger and little finger are deeply bent, leaving the thumb and forefinger to assume the so-called scissors shape. In action the middle finger and thumb are thrust against your opponent's throat and it is also possible to use the scissors of the thumb and forefinger to choke your opponent.

Hand techniques comprise tsukite or thrusting hand, tegatana or handsword, nukite or piercing hand, ukete or defending hand, haraite or sweeping hand. These methods are described below :

a. Ukete or Defence Hand : This method is used as a defence against an enemy's hand or leg attack. It is classified into several branches such as the jodan-uke, meaning literally the upper-step defence, but for practical purposes the upper body; the chudan-uke, middle-step or middle body defence; and the gedan-uke, lower-step or lower body defence.

Every uke is further divided into uchi-uke or inner uke and sotouke or outer uke, also termed omoto-uke and ura-uke. To this category also pertain numerous variants. For example, there are the ude-uke or arm-uke in which the fist is half clenched, the tegatana-uke or handsword uke in which the four fingers are stretched and the thumb bent for defence, the yoko-uke or lateral uke.

b. Tsukite or Thrusting Hand : This together with ukete is the most frequently utilized form of Tewaza. The hand should be instantly withdrawn after delivery of the thrust to avert the risk of being countered.

c. Yumi-Uke or Bow Uke : In this method, by means of the bow fist, you spring up your assailant's thrusting hand from underneath and so ward off his attack. This is also a type of ukete.

d. Haraite or Sweeping Hand : This is one kind of ukete in which you defend yourself by beating off an opponent's hand or leg attack. There are also the sub-divisions called the uchi-barai, the tegatana-barai.

e. Dakite or Hugging Hand : A kind of ukete. You grasp your opponent's thrusting hand, pull it towards you and under your arm but afterwards attack in your turn.

f. Uchite or Striking Hand : This method is used for both attack and defence. For example, in attack, you can use the hammer fist, handsword, to hit your opponent's vital spots. Or in defence, you can again use the hammer fist, the wrist or the handsword to strike his attacking hand or foot and so shatter his offensive power.

g. Kakete or Hook Hand : This is a type of ukete whereby you intercept an opponent's hand thrust.

h. Hikite or Pull Hand : This is a variant of the hook hand. The instant you parry your opponent's thrusting hand, you grasp his hand and pull it towards you. The pull hand enables you to disturb your opponent's posture, thus blocking his offensive and rendering your counter-attack more efficacious.

i. Sukuite or Scooping Hand : A kind of ukete whereby you scoop up your opponent's hand or leg and perhaps throw him. His attacking hand and leg are blocked and his posture is disturbed.

j. Hinerite or Twisting Hand : This is a variant of the hikite. However, you do not simply pull your opponent towards you but whilst twisting him in the opposite direction you also attack him.

Cuts with Edge of the Hand

Here sweeps with the open hand are discussed which aim at the softer parts of the opponent's body. It should be borne in mind that the decision whether to use the open hand or the fist can be made at the very last moment. For example, you might well use an upward sweep to the throat with the open hand, but should it become obvious that you are going to make contact with the side of the jaw it will be better to clench the fist, making contact with the little finger side. In this way, you will be far less likely to damage your own hand and the blow is made more effective.

Below various movements have been discussed which you can use against your opponent's attack with the edge of your hand.

Movement A

From the basic posture, step forward with the left foot, keeping the right fist at the right hip. The left hand, fingers straight and together, is taken up to the level of the left shoulder and slashed outwards and downwards. Return to basic posture.

Purpose—This movement could be used to ward-off a right-handed blow or to attack the left side of the opponent's body.

Movement B

Step forward with the right foot keeping the left fist at the left hip and taking the right arm, open handed, to the level of the left shoulder. The right arm then sweeps downwards and outwards. Return to the basic posture.

Purpose—This move is used to ward-off a left-handed blow or to cut at the right side of the opponent's body.

Movement C

Step to the left with the left foot, turning on the right, keeping the right fist at the hip and cutting upwards and outwards with the little finger edge of the left hand and forearm. Return to basic posture.

Purpose—This blow is used either to ward-off an attack or to deliver a cut to the opponent's left side or stomach.

Movement D

Step forward with the left foot, holding the right fist at the right hip. The left hand, fingers open, is taken close to the left hip and then, little finger edge leading, delivers a cut straight forward and a little upward to the opponent's groin or stomach. Resume the basic posture.

Purpose—The cut is delivered as if you were attempting to cut an opponent's body into two straight up through the middle.

Movement E

Step to the left with the left foot, pivoting on the right foot, holding the right fist at the right hip and having taken the left hand rear to the right shoulder cut outwards and downwards, little finger edge leading. Return to basic posture.

<u>Purpose</u>—The blow is used either to ward-off a blow aimed at you or to cut at the opponent's left side or stomach.

Movement F

Step forward with the left foot, holding the right fist at the right hip and sweeping from the level of the waist upwards and outwards with the left arm, open handed, and with the little finger edge leading. Return to the basic posture.

<u>Purpose</u>—This movement wards-off a right-handed blow to your head or upper body or cuts at the opponent's left armpit or neck.

Movement G

Stepping to your left with your left foot, turning on your right, keep your right fist at the hip and from close to your own right hip sweep forward and upward with the little finger cutting edge of the your left hand and forearm to the opponent's groin or lower stomach. Return to the basic posture.

Movement H

Advance the right foot, retaining the left fist at the left hip and taking the right hand, fingers straight, close to the left hip. The right arm, little finger edge of the hand and forearm leading, sweeps forward and a little upward cutting to the opponent's groin or stomach. Return to basic posture.

Movement I

Step to the right with the right foot, pivoting on the left, keeping the left fist at the hip. The right hand, fingers straight, sweeps from near your left hip upward and forward to the opponent's groin or lower part of the stomach. Return to the basic posture.

Movement J

Step to your right with your right foot, turning on your

left, and retaining your left fist at your hip deliver an upward and outward cut from the vicinity of the left hip with the little finger edge of the right forearm. Resume the basic posture.

Purpose—This cut may ward-off a blow or attack the opponent's stomach or right side.

Movement K

Step to the right with the right foot, turning on the left, holding the left fist at the left hip and cutting outward and downward from shoulder level with the right hand, fingers straight and little finger edge leading. Return to basic posture.

Use of Fist and Wrist

The defence and counter-attacks require the use of the weight of the fist and wrist as opposed to the grace of the edge of the hands, bludgeon instead of rapier. It may well be that they are more effective against clothed opponents, and certainly the blow delivered carries more weight.

On the other hand, there are occasions when the clenched fist is not so effective. This is so, for example, when the blow is to the throat and certainly it is not as easy to grab the attacker's clothing to draw him into a counter-blow when the clenched fist is used as when the attack is warded-off with the open hand.

Here different methods are mentioned which you can use when your opponent aims a blow to your face with his fist.

Attack A

You have to ward off a left-hand blow.

Steps—Step forward from the basic posture with the right foot.

-At the same time, take the right arm upward and outward, warding off the blow with the right wrist.

-Resume the basic posture.

Attack B

Movement is to ward-off a right-hand blow.

Steps—With your left foot, step forward from the basic posture, at the same time taking your left arm upward and outward, bending your left elbow with the back of the clenched hand facing outward.

-The blow is warded away with the left wrist. Return to the basic posture.

-Always use the wrist to ward-off.

Attack C

A right-handed punch is made to the middle of your body.

Steps—From the basic posture, step forward with the left foot, driving outward and downward with your left arm, fist clenched.

-The elbow is bent, with the back of the hand facing outward.

-The blow is warded-off with the left wrist. Resume the basic posture.

Attack D

An attack is made to the head with the right fist from your left side.

Steps—Step to your left from the basic posture, turning on your right foot to enable you to do so, at the same time driving your left fist upward and outward to ward-off the blow. Resume the basic posture.

Attack E

A right hand blow is aimed at your middle body from your left.

Steps—From the basic posture, step to your left with your left foot, turning on your right.

-Resume the basic posture.

Attack F

A left-hand punch to the head or chest from your right side is made by the attacker's left fist.

Steps—Step to the right, with the right foot, turning the left foot a little to the right to allow you to do so comfortably.

-At the same time, sweep upward and outward with the right arm, warding-off the attack.

-Blow is warded-off with the wrist.

Attack G

A left-handed blow is made which aims at your chest or head from your right.

Steps—Pivot on your left foot, step to your right with your right foot, and sweep your right fist and arm upward and outward to ward-off the blow.

-At the same time, drive the left fist into the middle of the attacker's body, stepping forward with the left foot if necessary.

-Return to the Basic Posture.

Attack H

A right-hand punch is aimed at your face or head.

Steps—From the basic posture, step forward with the left foot and ward-off the blow with an outward and upward sweep of your left fist and arm.

-As the left arm sweeps upwards, the right fist is driven into the middle of the opponent's body. You can step forward with the right foot, as the counter-punch is made, if necessary.

-Resume the basic posture.

Attack I

A left-hand blow is aimed at your middle body.

Steps—From the basic posture, step forward with your right foot, driving your right fist outward and downward to ward-off the blow.

-Again the elbow is bent and contact made with your right wrist, the back of which is turned outwards.

-Return to the basic posture.

Attack J

A left-handed blow is aimed at your middle body from your right.

Steps—Step to your right from the basic posture with your right foot, turning on your left foot as you do so warding-off the blow with your right wrist as you drive it outward and downward.

-Return to basic posture.

Attack K

Attacker aims a left-handed punch at the middle of your body from your front.

Steps—Sweep your right fist and arm outward and downward to ward-off the attack stepping forward with your right foot as you do so.

-At the same time, drive your left fist into the middle of the opponent's body or at his head, stepping forward if required with your left foot.

-Resume the basic posture.

Attack L

Attacker aims a right-hand punch to your head or face from your front.

Steps—Ward-off the blow by stepping forward with your left foot and sweeping your left fist and arm upwards and outwards.

-Take your right fist from your hip to a position close to your left hip and with the fist clenched, sweep upwards and a little to your right driving the right side of your fist, the little finger side, against the right side of the opponent's face or jaw.

-You should step forward with your right foot as you deliver the counter-blow.

Attack M

Attacker aims a right-handed blow to your middle body from your front.

Steps—Sweep downwards with the left fist and arm, keeping the elbow slightly bent and stepping forward with your left foot as you do.

-At the same time, counter with a right-handed blow to the stomach, advancing your right foot if necessary.

Attack N

A left-hand punch is aimed at your head or upper body.

Steps—Step forward with your right foot from the basic posture, warding-off the blow with an upward and outward sweep of your right fist and arm.

-As the blow is warded-off, drive your left fist into the opponent's middle body, stepping forward with the left foot, if necessary.

-Resume the basic posture.

Attack O

Attacker aims a right-hand blow to your head or face from your left side.

Steps—Pivoting on your right foot, step to your left side,

warding-off the attack with an upward and outward sweep of your left fist and arm.

-As you ward-off the blow, drive your right fist to the middle of the opponent's body, stepping forward with the right foot if required.

-Resume the basic posture.

Attack P

A left-handed punch is made to your face or head from your front.

Steps—From the basic posture, step forward with your right foot, sweeping upward and outward with your right arm and fist to ward-off the blow with your right wrist, at the same time taking your left fist across your body from your left to the vicinity of your right hip.

-Stepping forward with your left foot, drive your left fist across your body and upwards to strike the left side of his head or jaw with the little finger side of your fist.

-Return to basic posture.

Attack Q

A right-handed blow is made to your middle body from your left side.

Steps—Turning on your right foot, step to your left and ward-off the blow with a downward and outward sweep of your left fist and arm.

-Counter by stepping forward with your right foot and driving your right fist to his middle body or head.

-Resume the basic posture.

Attack R

A right-hand blow is made to the face aimed at you from your right side.

Steps—Pivot on your left foot to your right, stepping to your right with your right foot and sweeping the blow away with an upward and outward sweep of your left fist and arm.

-Counter by stepping forward with your left foot and driving your right fist into your opponent's middle body.

-Resume the basic posture.

Attack S

Attacker aims a left-handed punch to your face from your left side.

<u>Steps</u>—Pivot to your left on your right foot, advancing your left foot and sweeping outwards and upwards with your right fist and arm.

-Advancing the right foot, drive your left fist to your opponent's middle body.

-Resume the basic posture.

EMPI HIJIATE, or Elbow Attacks

In karate the elbow is used to assail your opponent's solar-plexus, chest and abdomen.

a. Sageta Empi or Lowered Empi : In this posture, your elbows are held downwards in readiness for attack or hijiate.

b. Tate-Empi or Vertical Empi : In this posture, you stand with your fists touching your hip and your elbow held upwards. If both elbows are held upwards, then the technical term is ryo-tate-empi or both-vertical-empi.

c. Ko-Empi or Rear Empi : This is one of the most frequently used methods of an elbow attack or hijiate. The first is brought up about as far as the ear but then apparently lowered, it touches the hip in such wise that if you happen to be hugged from behind by your opponent, you can drive your elbow with maximum force into his solar-plexus.

d. Zengo Empi or Front and Rear Empi : When attacked by two opponents from the front and rear respectively, you bring both your left and right elbows into play apparently against the solar-plexus.

e. Zen Empi or Frontal Empi : The fist is held close to the back of the head as if in the act of carrying something, and for attack the elbow is brought forward.

f. Hineri-Yoko-Empi or Twisting-Lateral-Empi : In this method, both fists are held with the thumb edges at the side of both breasts and the elbow opened. The shoulders should not be spread but kept well lowered.

In this posture the upper part of your body can be twisted to the right or left and your right or left elbow used simultaneously against the solar-plexus of an enemy attacking from the side or rear. It may be possible to have recourse to this method if attacked by very strong opponents.

g. Yoko-Empi or Lateral Empi : In this method the right or left fist and elbow are held horizontally; then brought in front of the chest in order to deliver a lateral elbow attack. If both elbows are used the method is called ryo-yoko-empi.

The elbows are valuable weapons particularly when you are beside your opponent. They can be more useful than the knee which, although it delivers a far heavier blow, tends to be rather restricted for other than frontal attacks. As most blows are delivered to the front or back, it is seldom realised how vulnerable the sides of the head, body and thigh are to attack.

Attack A

The attacker aims a left-handed blow to your head or upper body.

Step I—Step forward to his left side with your right foot, wardering-off the blow with an upwards and outwards sweep of your right arm. As your right foot is replaced on the mat, take the left foot past the outside of his left foot and taking the left fist above the right shoulder, drive your elbow outwards to the side of his body.

Alternatively, you can step forward between his feet with your left foot and counter with an upward drive of the left knee to his groin.

Step II—Step to his left side with your right foot, warding-off his blow with an upward and outward sweep of your right arm. Immediately, you replace your right foot on the ground, step outside the attacker's left foot with your left foot and taking your left fist above your right shoulder, drive the elbow outwards to the side of his neck. Alternatively, instead of moving your left foot outside his left foot, step with it between his feet and deliver a blow to his groin with your left knee as a second counter-attack.

Attack B

Your opponent attacks with his right arm to your head or upper body.

Step I—Step forward to the opponent's right side with the left foot, warding-off the blow with an upwards and outwards sweep of the left arm, fingers extended. As soon as your left foot returns to the ground, step forward with the right foot, taking it to your left to the opponent's right foot and drive your right elbow outwards to the side of his body.

To attack with the right elbow, the right hand is taken back to the top of the left shoulder in order to develop maximum power for the blow. To this, counter can be added a blow with the right knee. Instead of advancing your right foot outside that of your opponent, step between your opponent's feet with the right foot driving the knee up into his groin following up with the elbow to the body.

Step II—Advance the left foot to the opponent's left side, warding-off the blow with an upward and outward sweep with your left arm. As the left foot is placed on the ground, advance the right past the outside of the opponent's right foot and taking the right fist up above the right shoulder, drive the elbow outwards and downwards into the side of the attacker's neck.

Again, there is the alternative of bringing the right foot between the opponent's feet and driving the knee upwards into his groin, as the elbow drives into his neck.

Attack C

The attacker grips you from behind round your arms and body. Bend your knees to lower your body and drive your elbow outwards and upwards. This loosens, or may even break, the grip round your arms.

Turn a little to your right and drive your right elbow backwards into the middle of the attacker's body. You could equally well turn to your left and drive the left elbow backwards into his body. .

Attack D

You are attacked with a right-handed blow to the head or upper body from your right side.

Step I—As the punch is delivered, step to your right with your right foot, warding-off the blow with an upward and out-ward sweep of your right arm.

46

As the right foot is replaced on the mat, step to your original right with your left foot, taking it in front of and across your right. Taking the right fist close to the right shoulder, deliver an outward blow to the side or back of the opponent's body with left elbow.

Step II—The same as in the earlier step, however, after moving your left foot in front of and across your right, drive your right knee upwards into the outside of your opponent's right thigh. Should he not have turned sufficiently to his left to enable you to do this, drive the knee into his groin.

Attack E

Step I—You are held from behind by an opponent who throws his arm round your neck and pulls you backwards. Do not worry too much about being pulled back but turn to your right, pushing your hips back as you make the turn. You will find that as your turn is completed, you will have recovered balance.

The turn continues until you have your right side towards your opponent, when you drive your right elbow into his right side. To deliver the blow, the right fist should be taken across the body and above the left shoulder in order to develop power for the counter-attack.

Step II—This is identical to step I, except that you turn to your left and deliver the blow with the elbow with your left arm to his left side. It does not matter which way you turn when you are held round the neck from behind.

It may be better to turn right when it is the opponent's left arm which is round your neck and to your left when he uses his right, but this makes very little difference. In addition, you may not be able to tell which arm is being used. The main object must be to move rapidly. There is no point in passing out whilst you consider which way to turn.

Attack F

The attacker grips you round the body from behind, but

leaves your arms free. In this position, you cannot reach him with your arms or elbows so you have to loose his grip.

To do this, raise both your arms forward, with the knuckles facing downwards and drive your fists down onto the backs of his forearms, hands or wrists. The blow is delivered with the knuckles of the fore and middle fingers.

As he loosens his grip, turn a little to the right and drive your right elbow upwards into the side of his head or downwards into the middle or side of his body. Alternatively, turn to the left and make a similar attack to his left side with your left elbow. To attack with the elbow, the fist is taken up above the opposite shoulder before it is driven into the opponent.

PUNCHES

Choku Tzuki or Chudan

This is one of the important technique which every performer should learn carefully.

Technique

For this, you have to stand with the feet hip-width apart facing forwards and parallel. The knees should be slightly bent. Extend the left hand in line with the sternum, with the wrist bent so that the fingers point upwards and the little finger faces forward.

The right fist should be drawn back over the right hip, with the elbow tucked in and the wrist straight. Pull the left hand back towards the hip and simultaneously propel the right hand out. At the half-way point, both elbows should brush against the rib cage so that the fists move in a straight line.

Arms should work together with an equal and opposite action. When the right elbow leaves the rib cage and starts to move forward, the elbow should be rotated. Pull the shoulders down and lock the arm out with the muscles of the arm and shoulder.

If the elbow has been correctly rotated a very slight bend should remain in the arm, with a few centimetres of movement left by the time focus is reached. On no account should the arm be locked straight, with bone against bone. The first two knuckles of the punching fist should be in line with the sternum. The wrist should be straight and not cocked up or down. Little finger should be tightly rolled in order to tense the tendon on the outside of the arm.

At the point of kimae, breathe out. Push the head and chest up at the same time. The hip of the punching side moves slightly forward and the muscles of the hip, buttock and stomach should simultaneously lock as hard as possible. The body should have complete muscular connection throughout at the point of focus.

After a period of constant practice, this should produce a vibration throughout the body. If a jarring sensation occurs, the muscles are not all being tensed in the correct unison. This jarring can cause stress to various parts of the body, particularly the shoulders, chest and spine.

Gyaku Tzuki

Technique

The left hand should be raised in line with the sternum and the head and eyes forward. The right elbow should be pulled back tightly and the shoulders kept down in a similar position to choku tuzik, only with a difference that this time body should be half-facing.

The chin should be relaxed and kept in, not sticking forwards, as this can make a difference to the control factor as you punch. Keep the back straight and relaxed and the hips at an angle of 45°, making sure that from the hip width position the body is maintained within the extremities of the foot position.

Keep the front knee bent; the big toe should be turned one toe's distance inside towards the centre line of the body. The rear knee should be twisted out as much as possible, which puts pressure on the rear foot and helps to keep it flat as long as the rear foot is at an angle of 45°.

While executing this movement, the actual punch is basically the same as choku tzuki, except that the gyaku tzuki has the propulsion of the hips and the spring-loading of the rear leg against the floor adding force and momentum to it. As the punch is executed, the front arm is drawn back and the rear arm simultaneously moves forwards until both elbows are squeezing the lower ribs.

At this point, slightly relax the rear leg and hip, then twist the hip and rotate the whole of the rear leg, so that the knee has rotated through a quarter circle towards the ground. The foot should remain still.

Push the right hip forward as far as possible, but keep the left hip relaxed, drawn down and slightly back. The front knee will move slightly forwards at this stage, but do not let it move out to the left. The inner thigh muscles are then locked as the right arm is fully extended, with a half rotation of the elbow, and the left hand is pulled back.

The stomach, buttocks and the whole body should be focused simultaneously. It is better to allow the whole body to move slightly forward rather than trying to counteract this by taking the shoulders and the body back, since this could have a detrimental effect on the lumbar region. At the point of kimae, there should be a vibrational effect, not a jarring sensation, throughout the body. The muscle of the hip and leg should be relaxed slightly and then twisted forwards and kimaed without any compacting of the joints.

You should neither hyperextend the joint nor push against it. In a correct gyaku tzuki, the rear knee is rolled in so that the hips, facing forwards, are locked against each other and the student has full use of all the muscle groups.

Attacks on Body and Head

Here different kinds of attack and the manner in which you have to tackle them is mentioned step by step.

Attack A

A defence against a blow with foot or arm aimed at the lower part of your body.

Step I—Attacker aims a blow at the lower part of your body with his right hand. Step forward with the left leg, raising the left arm towards your right shoulder and then dashing your arm, with the fist clenched, down-wards and outwards, making contact with the little finger edge of the fist or forearm. The right fist is retained at the right hip.

Step II—Advance the right foot, driving the right fist down into the lower part of the opponent's body, probably his stomach or solar-plexus. The left fist is withdrawn to the left hip. Return to the basic posture.

Attack B

A defence against a blow or kick to your middle body is made by the opponent.

Step I—From the basic posture, raise your left hand towards your right shoulder and stepping forward with your left foot, sweep your left arm downward and outward with your fist clenched.

Alternatively, the edge of the hand can be used. Your right fist remains at your right hip. The opponent's right arm or leg is dashed away with the little finger edge of your fist or forearm.

Step II—As the attacker's blow is dashed away, step forward with the right leg and drive your right fist straight forward to the opponent's chest or face. The left fist is taken back to the left hip. Return to the basic posture.

Step III—To defend against a left-handed or left-footed blow to the body, step forward with the right foot, raising the right arm to the left shoulder and dashing the blow away with the little finger edge of your forearm, hand or clenched fist. The left fist remains at the left hip.

Step IV—Step forward with the left leg, driving the left fist to the opponent's chest or face. The right fist is returned to the right hip. Return to the basic posture.

Attack C

Attack comes from the rear in the form of a kick or blow to the lower part of the body. In the defence and counter-attack you have to make a complete about turn. The attack is made with the right arm.

Step I—From the basic posture, you pivot on your right foot turning to your left and stepping forward a pace to what was, from your basic posture, your rear. Your left hand is taken to your right shoulder and swept downwards and outwards to ward-off the attacker's blow. The little finger edge of the fist and forearm make contact. The right fist remains at the right hip.

Step II—You now take your right leg past your left, taking the left fist back to the left hip and driving your right fist down into the opponent's stomach. Return to the basic posture.

Step III—This time, the attack is made against you with the opponent's left arm. From the basic posture, pivot to the right on the left foot stepping to your original rear with your right foot. At the same time, you raise your right hand to your left shoulder and sweep it downwards and outwards to ward-off the blow. Your left fist is retained at your left hip.

Step IV—Complete the turn by stepping to your original rear with your left foot and driving your left fist to the middle of the opponent's body.

The right fist is taken down to the right hip. Then resume the basic posture.

Attack D

Attack is developed from your left. The blow against which you defend is delivered to the lower or middle part of the body with a fist cr foot.

Step I—From the basic posture, step to your left with your left foot, holding on your right fist at your hip and raising your left hand to your right shoulder to dash it downwards and outwards to ward-off the blow. The contact is made with the little finger edge of the fist or forearm.

Step II—Take your right foot past your left, driving your right fist to your opponent's face or chest and taking the left fist back to your left hip. Resume the basic posture.

Attack E

Attack from the right.

Steps—Pivot to the right on the right foot stepping to your original right with the left foot. At the same time, retain the left fist at the left hip and drive the right fist to the opponent's stomach. Return to the basic posture.

Attack F

An attack is made from the left.

Steps—Step to your left with your left foot pivoting on your right to do so. At the same time, hold the right fist at the right hip and bring the left fist up to the vicinity of the right shoulder sweeping it downwards and outwards to ward-off a blow to the middle or lower part of your body. The ward-off is made with the little finger edge of the fist or forearm. Return to the basic posture.

Attack G

An attack is made from right.

Steps—From the basic posture, pivot to the right on the left foot, taking the right foot a pace to the right. At the same time, hold the left fist at the right hip and drive the right fist to the middle of the opponent's body. Return to the basic posture.

Attack H

To ward-off an attack from the rear.

Steps—Make a complete left about turn to the left on the right foot, stepping to the new front with the left foot as you do so. At the same time hold the right fist at the right hip and sweep the left arm outwards and downwards to ward-off a right-handed blow to the lower or middle body. The left fist should be taken to the vicinity of the right shoulder before the sweep commences. Return to the basic posture.

Attack I

When an attack is made from the rear.

Steps—Pivot to the right on left foot, stepping round with your right foot to your new front. Simultaneously, hold the left fist at the left hip and take your right fist to the level of the left shoulder. At once, sweep it outwards and downwards to ward-off an attack to the lower or middle body with the opponent's left fist or foot. Return to the basic posture.

Attack J

When an attack from the left.

Steps—Pivot to your left on the right foot, stepping to the left with the left foot. This time, hold the left fist at the left hip and taking the right fist to the left shoulder, sweep with it outwards and downwards to ward-off a left-hand blow to the middle or lower body. The little finger edge of the fist and forearm lead and make contact. Resume the basic posture.

Attack K

When an attack is made from the right.

Steps—Step to your right with your left foot, pivoting on your right foot to do so. As you pivot, retain the left fist at the left hip at the same time taking the right fist to the left shoulder and sweeping it downwards and outwards as if to ward-off a blow to the middle or lower part of the body. The ward-off is made with the little finger edge of the fist or forearm. Return to the basic posture.

Attack L

An attack is made from the rear.

Steps—To ward-off a left-handed blow or kick to your lower or middle body, turn to the left on the right foot, stepping back with your left foot. At the same time, the left fist is held at the left hip and the right arm is swept downwards and outwards from shoulder level to ward-off the left-handed attack. The ward-off is made with the little finger edge of the fist and forearm. Resume the basic posture.

Attack M

Attack is made from the rear.

Steps—Pivot to the right on the left foot stepping back to your original rear with the right foot. Simultaneously, hold the right fist at the right hip and taking the left fist to the level of your right shoulder, sweep downwards and outwards with your left arm, little finger edge leading, to ward-off a right-hand blow aimed at your middle or lower body. Return to the basic posture.

Attack N

When an attack is made from right.

Steps—Pivot to the right on the left foot, stepping to the right with the right foot, retaining the right fist at the right hip and from shoulder level sweeping outwards and downwards with the left fist and forearm, little finger edge leading. This is to ward-off a right-handed attack to the lower or middle part of the body. Return to the basic posture.

Tackling Kicks and Blows from the Knee

A kick, together with an attack with the knee always appears to be a form of attack which is far more frightening than the danger resulting from it really merits. These attacks are almost always made to the groin or stomach and should they land there is no doubt that the victim would be disabled and be at the mercy of his opponent.

However, as the target is in the front of the body, it is not difficult to ward-off such an attack by a simple twist of the hips. The blow, even the ward-off fail, will land comparatively harmlessly in the hip area.

All movements should be commenced from the basic posture and you must return to this basic posture on completion of each movement. This ensures that as well as having turned the side of the body to the attacker, you also have the hand not in use free and well positioned to deal with a kick or drive of the knee to your body. Failure to return to the basic posture can leave you open to subsequent attacks.

Here various kinds of attacks and methods of warding-off and countering kicks and blows with the knee have been discussed step by step.

Attack A

You are attacked with a left-footed kick to your groin.

Steps—Stepping forward with your right foot, take your right fist up to the vicinity of your left chest and then drive the arm downwards and outwards, sweeping the leg away past your right side with either a hammer-fist or side-hand blow. Return to the basic posture.

Attack B

Your opponent attacks by kicking to your groin with his right foot.

Steps—From the basic posture, take your left fist across your body to the vicinity of the right side of your chest and sweep downwards and outwards to your left to ward-off the kick. Make contact with the fist or edge of the hand, whichever you consider more effective.

As you take your left arm across your body, advance your left foot so that your left hip faces the kick. Should your defensive sweep with your left arm fail, the kick will then only strike your hip or thigh. The sweep is aimed at the inside calf of the leg or the inside thigh, depending on how close you are to the opponent. Either blow will cause severe pain should it land on its target.

Attack C

Attacker aims a left-foot kick to your groin.

Steps—Raise your right foot and bending your right knee, drive the outside of your foot down against the opponent's shin as he kicks upwards. At once return to the basic posture.

Attack D

Attacker drives his right knee upwards and forwards into your groin.

Steps—It is impossible to sweep this form of attack away with an arm so your own leg has to be used. As the attack is delivered, move your left leg forward, and bending your leg at the knee, drive the knee to your right so that it strikes the outside of the attacker's knee or thigh. Resume the basic posture.

Not only will this defence succeed in protection you, but it may also disable the opponent's leg.

Attack E

The opponent kicks at your groin with his right foot.

Step I—Advance your left leg, sweeping the attacking leg downwards and outwards with your left arm. Now counter-attack by kicking forwards and upwards to his groin with your right foot, making contact with your instep. Return to basic posture.

Step II—The right-footed kick to your groin, step in with your left foot, sweeping outwards and downwards with your left arm. This time, as you sweep away the attacking leg slide your left hand under his leg and lift his leg outwards and upwards so stretching his legs outwards.

At once, drive your right foot upwards and forwards into his groin which is now fully exposed to your kick. Return to basic posture.

Attack F

Your attacker attempts to drive his left knee into your groin or stomach.

Step I—Bend your right leg and drive the knee across your body into the outside of his knee or thigh. Without a break in your movement, continue the drive of your knee upwards or repeat the drive upwards into his left side or the base of his spine. Return to basic posture.

Step II—You are attacked by the opponent's left knee which is aimed at your groin or stomach. Defend by bending your right leg and driving the knee across your body into the outside of his knee or thigh. At once, replace your right foot on the ground and counter by bending your left leg and driving your left knee upwards and forwards into the attacker's groin. Return to the basic posture.

Attack G

You are attacked with a left-footed kick to your groin.

Step I—Meet his kick by bending your left knee and driving the outside of your left foot down and forward against his shin as he kicks upwards.

Immediately, ensuring that the toes of your left foot are pointed downwards to add to the power of your movement, bend your left knee fully and drive the knee upwards and forwards into the attacker's groin or stomach. Return to basic posture.

Step II—Again meet his left-footed kick by bending your left knee and driving the outside edge of your left foot down onto his shin as he makes his kick. Immediately, you make your contact with his shin withdraw your leg a little and kick upwards to his groin with the left leg, making contact with your instep. Return to basic posture.

Attack H

Attacker aims a right-footed kick to your groin.

Step I—Lift your right foot, warding-off the kick by bending your right knee and driving the outside of your right foot forwards and downwards against his shin as he kicks upwards.

As soon as you have made contact with his shin, drive your right knee upward into his groin or stomach. Resume the basic posture.

Step II—Against the same right-footed kick, defend by blocking with the outside of your right foot but instead of countering with a counter-blow with your knee to his groin withdraw your right foot and kick upward to his groin, making contact with the instep of your right foot. Resume the basic posture.

Attack I

Attacker aims a left-foot kick to your groin.

Step I—Step forward with your right foot, sweeping outwards and downwards with your right arm to ward-off the attack. At once, counter with a left-foot kick to your opponent's groin and then resume the basic posture.

Step II—Again you are attacked with a left-foot kick to the groin which is warded-off by stepping forward with the right foot and sweeping outwards and downwards with the right arm.

This time, you ward-off slide your right hand under the attacker's left leg and lift it upwards and outwards thus spreading him out so that he is really open to a counter-kick to his groin with your left foot. Resume the basic posture.

Attack J

The opponent attempts to drive his right knee to your groin.

Step I—This attack is warded-off by bending the left leg and driving your leg knee upwards and across your body so that your knee makes contact with the outside of his right knee or thigh.

At once, repeat or continue the drive of your left knee into the base of his spine or right side. Resume the basic posture.

Step II—Ward-off an attack to your groin with your opponent's right knee by bending your own left knee and driving it across your body into the outside of the attacker's knee or thigh.

At once, replace your left foot on the ground and counter-attack by driving your right knee upwards and forwards into the opponent's groin, stomach or left side. Resume the basic posture.

Dealing with Repeated or Successive Attacks

You may well have to deal with several successive blows before the opportunity is provided for your counter. Similarly, you may have to deliver more than one blow against your opponent before he is rendered unable to continue his attack. In free practice, you stimulate a fight in which all Karate movements are used, but the blows are pulled just short of their target. Each contestant is expected to called out 'Maitta', that is 'I am beaten' in acknowledgment of a blow which would have landed.

Attack A

The attack is made with successive left and right punches to the head.

Step I—The left arm is warded-off with an outward and upward sweep of the right arm, fingers extended, stepping in with the right foot.

The right hand punch, which follows is deflected with a similar sweep of the left arm, step in with the left foot if space permits. The attacker has now both of his arms pushed outwards and upwards, and you counter by turning the left wrist anti-clockwise and attacking at his neck with the little finger side of the fist.

Step II—The attack is warded-off in exactly the same manner with outward and upward sweeps of the right and left arms. This time, as the second blow is warded-off, do not step in but instead, drive the left knee into the attacker's groin.

Attack B

The opponent attacks with a right-handed blow to the head or upper body followed by a left-handed blow to the same target.

Step I—As the opponent punches with his right hand,

step in with the left foot and ward-off the blow with an upwards and outwards sweep of the left arm, fingers extended. The left hand blow is avoided by a similar upward and outward sweep of the right arm, stepping in with the right foot if there is space. To counter, turn the right arm anti-clockwise and drive the little finger side of the left hand down to the right side of his neck.

An alternative to this is to clench the left fist and by turning it anti-clockwise, deliver a hammer-fist blow with the little finger side of the fist to the top of the opponent's head or his right temple.

Step II—The two punches are warded-off in the manner described earlier, but this time, do not step in with the right foot and instead of using the right arm to counter-attack, you drive your right knee into the attacker's groin.

Attack C

You meet the drive of the opponent's knee at your groin. At close quarters, this is a very difficult attack to deflect especially should it be a second attack made when your attention is concentrated on the first.

This is the case in this defence in which your opponent drives his right fist to your head and follows up with his knee to your body. Which knee does not matter particularly as defence is the same.

Step I—Ward-off the right-hand punch to the head by stepping forward with your left foot and sweeping upwards and outwards with your left arm, keeping the fingers extended.

Now as the attacker drives one of his knees up to your body, bring your own left knee upwards and to your right so that the point of your knee meets the side of the attacker's knee or leg. This not only wards-off the blow but also disables his leg. Now step in with your right foot and drive your right knee to the opponent's groin.

Step II—This is exactly the same as for step I in that you

ward-off the blow and drive off the knee attack with your own left knee. At this stage, instead of countering with your right knee, you clench your right fist and, stepping in with your right foot, drive your right fist to the middle of his body.

Attack D

The attacker punches to the head or upper body with his right arm and follows up with a left-handed punch to the stomach.

Step I—The punch to the head with the right hand is warded-off with an upward and outward sweep of the left arm, the fingers being extended. You should step in as you ward-off this blow.

The left-hand punch to the stomach is warded-off with a downward and outward sweep of the right arm, the fingers of which are also extended. Step in with the right foot if there is room. Your left arm is not turned anti-clockwise and the little finger edge of the hand is swept down across the right side of his neck.

As an alternative, the left fist can be clenched and the little finger side of the fist crashed down on the attacker's head or temple in hammer-fist fashion.

Step II—The right-arm punch to the head and left-arm punch to the stomach are warded-off as in the earlier step with successive sweeps of the left and right arms. As before, you step in with the left foot as you sweep away his blow to the head with your left arm, but this time, as you ward-off, the left-hand punch to the stomach you hold the leg back, driving your right knee into the attacker's groin.

Attack E

You are attacked with successive blows. The first a left-hand punch to the head and the second a right-hand punch to the stomach.

Step I—The left-handed punch to the head is warded-off

with an upward and outward sweep with the right arm, fingers extended. Step forward with the right foot as you make the sweep. As the second attack is made to the stomach with the right arm, deflect the attack with a downward and outward sweep with the left hand. Fingers should be extended.

Step in with the left foot as you sweep if there is space. Now turn your right wrist clockwise and sweep the little finger edge of the right hand down to the left side of the attacker's neck.

There are two alternatives. You can clench your right fist and crash the fist down to the opponent's head or temple. Contact should be made with the little finger edge of the fist. The second alternative is to clench the right fist and bending the arm at the elbow drive the right elbow and upper forearm to the attacker's face.

Step II—The successive punches are warded-off in exactly the way in the earlier step, but as you make the deflecting sweep with the left arm, you do not step in. Instead, you point the toes of your left foot downwards and drive your left knee upwards into the attacker's groin.

Attack F

Your opponent attacks with a left-handed punch to your face or upper body and follows up by attempting to drive his knee to your groin.

Step I—As the opponent delivers his left-handed punch, step in with your right foot, sweeping it upwards and outwards with your right arm to deflect the blow. Your fingers should be extended.

Now as he attacks at your body with his knee, drive your own right knee upwards and inwards, making contact with the side of his knee or leg. Now drive your left knee into the groin of your opponent.

Step II—As for the above step, you ward-off the left-handed attack to the head with an upward and outward sweep of your right hand, extending the fingers, and stepping in with your right foot as you do so.

Ward-off the knee attack by driving your own right knee upwards and inwards and immediately step in with your left foot, driving your left fist into his middle body.

Attack G

You are attacked with a left-handed blow to the stomach immediately followed by a right-handed punch to the head or upper body.

Step I—Ward-off the left-hand punch to the stomach by taking your right hand close to your left shoulder and then sweeping your arm outwards and downwards.

The second attack to your head with his right arm is warded-off with an upward and outward sweep of your left arm. At once bend your right arm, which has been returned to the basic position, at the elbow and counter with an upward drive of your elbow and forearm to the opponent's face.

Step II—Ward-off the blows as described in previous step. As a result, your right fist is placed low at your right side whilst your left is held above your left shoulder. Immediately, turn your left forearm anti-clockwise and deliver a sidehand cut down to the side of the opponent's neck.

Instead of the cut you can clench your left fist and deliver a hammer-fist blow to the side of his neck or the top of his head.

Attack H

Your assailant attempts to drive his right fist into your stomach and follows up with a left-handed blow to your head or upper body.

Step I—As your opponent drives his right fist to your stomach, ward it off with a downward and outward sweep of your left arm. This is made by taking your left fist from

65

your left hip to your right shoulder and commencing the sweep. As you sweep, step forward with your left foot. At once ward-off the left-hand punch to your head with an upwards and outwards sweep of your right arm. The result of these two defensive sweeps is to drive both his arms outwards, leaving your own arms in a good position inside his for a counter which he cannot ward-off.

At once counter-attack by driving your left arm, which having swept downwards, has been returned to its basic position, upwards to drive your elbow and forearm into his face; move in with your left foot as you do so if this is possible. As you stepped in with that foot in your original counter any further advance with it may not be possible. However, even a slight forward movement adds power to the blow.

Step II—The two successive blows are warded-off as in the earlier step, your left arm sweeping downwards and outwards and your right arm sweeping upwards and outwards. This time counter-attack by using your upraised right hand to deliver an edge of the hand blow with the little finger edge to the left of his neck.

As an alternative, you can clench your right fist and deliver a hammer-fist blow to the side or top of his head.

Step III—Again ward-off the successive right-and left-arm attacks with the defensive sweeps of your left arm downwards and outwards and your right outwards and upwards as fully described in above mentioned step. This time take advantage of the weak position by driving either knee upwards and forwards into his groin. The knee to be used will depend on the position of yourself and your opponent.

Attack I

The attacker attempts a right-footed kick to your groin and follows up with a right-handed punch to your head or upper body.

Step I—As the attacker delivers his upward right-footed

kick to your groin, sweep it away with a downwards and outwards sweep with the little finger edge of your left hand, keeping the fingers extended.

A hammer-fist blow would be equally effective, perhaps more so. This attack having failed, he replaces his foot on the ground and drives his right fist at your head. This is checked with an upward and outward sweep of your left arm. As this second defensive sweep of your left arm tends to straighten him, drive your right fist into his stomach or groin, stepping in with your right foot as you do so.

Step II—The attack is warded-off as in the earlier step. As the result of two successive attacks from his right foot and arm he should have his right leg well advanced. Take advantage of this by pointing the toes of your right foot downwards and driving your right knee upwards and forwards into his groin.

Step III—Ward-off the right-footed kick with a downward and outward sweep of your left arm. The punch to the head with the opponent's right arm is warded-off with an upward and outward blow with your left arm. Do not step in with your left foot.

This double attack from your opponent's right side leaves him turned to his left, thus providing the opportunity for a counter from your right side. Immediately take advantage of this and by kicking upwards and forwards, drive your right instep up into his groin.

Use of Clothing

Although the first objective of any means of defence must be to ward-off the attack, in Karate, you are provided with a series of devastating counter-attacks. Therefore, the hand and arm used to ward-off a blow need not be used for that purpose only, although the ward-off must come first.

Having warded-off, the hand can catch the opponent's arm or clothing and draw him on into a position for a far more effective counter. It is a serious mistake to attempt to catch the hand, arm or weapon with which the opponent attacks.

A defence in which the defender is attempting to ward-off a blow with his hand, greatly reduces the effectiveness of the defence and also provides a very good chance of the contact resulting in broken or dislocated fingers or thumb. Use the warding-off hand to catch the attacker's arm or clothing to draw him into the counter-blow. This either draws him into a more satisfactory position or adds power to the counter, in many cases both.

Opponent punches at your head with his right fist. You step forward with your left foot, sweeping your left arm, fingers outstretched, upwards and outwards. The blow is warded-off with the little finger edge of the forearm. At once, bend your left wrist and hand round the opponent's right arm from above so that you can grip his arm or sleeve. Now the attacker can be drawn forward in the direction of his punch without any break in his movement.

It will be found that in this way, not only is he drawn forward without difficulty, but he is also drawn towards your left side. This has the double effect of opening his left side to a counter-blow and making it very difficult for him to strike at you with his left arm. Initial ward-off does check the attacker's movement, but only deflects it. As a result the attacker's forward motion from the blow is continuous as you draw him forward. Any break in the movement results in the failure of the defender's own counteraction.

Counter-Attacks

Here various manners in which your opponent can attack and methods in which you have deal are given in detail.

Attack A

Your attacker drives his left fist to your head or upper body.

Step I—Ward-off the blow by sweeping upwards and

outwards with your right arm, extending the fingers and stepping in with the right foot as you do so.

Immediately, step in with your left foot and, bending your left arm at the elbow, drive your left elbow to his jaw, the forearm making contact with his face. This attack will bend his body backwards or at least he will lean back in an attempt to avoid it, so at once bend your left leg and pointing the toes drive your right knee forwards and upwards into his groin. Immediately, resume the basic posture.

Step II—Ward-off the left-hand blow to your head with an upwards and outwards sweep of your right arm. Extend your fingers and step in with the right foot as you do this. At once, counter-attack by stepping in with your left foot, and bending your left arm at the elbow drive the elbow and forearm upward and forward into his head, contacting his jaw with your elbow and his face with your forearm.

With your right fist which was returned to the basic posture, as soon as the initial blow was warded-off, punch to the opponent's left side or stomach. You can now continue the counter-attack by driving your left knee to his groin. Return to the basic posture.

Step III—Deflect the left-hand punch to the head by stepping in with your left foot, and taking your left fist across your body to your right hip sweep upwards and across to your left. Straighten the fingers as you do so. This will tend to turn the attacker to his right, so take advantage of this to step in with your right foot and drive your right fist into his side or back.

Immediately, bend your left leg and drive the knee upwards and forwards into the opponent's middle body or the base of his spine according to his position relative to yourself. Resume the basic posture.

Attack B

You are attacked with a right-handed blow at the head or

upper body·   •

Step I—As you are attacked, ward-off his right arm by sweeping your left arm with the fingers extended upwards and outwards. As you do so, step in with your left foot. Immediately, step in with your right foot and bending your right arm drive your right elbow and forearm upwards and forwards into your opponent's face and jaw.

The elbow should contact his jaw and your forearm drive against his face. Take advantage of the fact that the blow from your right elbow will drive his body backwards or make him bend back to avoid it, to bend your left knee and drive the knee upwards and forwards into his groin. Resume the basic posture.

Step II—Again ward-off the right-arm blow to the head or upper body with an upwards and outwards sweep of your left arm, extending the fingers of the hand as you do so and stepping in with your left foot. As in the first step, counter by stepping in with your right foot and bending your arm at the elbow, drive your right forearm and elbow to the opponent's head. Your elbow should make contact with his jaw and your forearm with his face. Drive your left fist, which should have been returned to its basic position immediately it had warded-off the initial blow, into the opponent's right side or stomach.

At this stage, you could follow up with a drive of your right knee to his groin. Return to the basic posture.

Step III—You are attacked with a right-hand blow to your head or upper body. This time step in with your right foot and taking your right hand across your body until it is close to your left hip sweep the attacker's blow away with an upward and outward sweep of your right arm with the fingers extended.

This ward-off will tend to turn the opponent to his left, so make use of this to step in with your left foot and drive your left fist into his side or back. Follow up by bending your right knee, and pointing the toes downward, drive your knee upward into the opponent's middle body or base of his spine depending on which way his body is turned at this stage. Resume basic posture.

Defence against Kicks

It is just as easy way to defend against kicks by stepping back as it is against blows with the fist. In fact, as the leg is a longer and more powerful weapon, it may well be better to do so. For the same reasons, the kicks are not always warded-off by the Karatemen with sweeps of the arm. Instead a cross-arm defence is used.

From the basic posture, the defender moves both arms inwards so that they cross in front of him and block the kick with the V formed between them. Contact is made with the little finger edges of the forearms. This is a solid block although by turning the hips the body may be turned so deflecting the attacker's leg to the left or the right, thus making the defence safer and more effective.

However, kicks are warded-off with sweeps of the arms in exactly the same manner as the blows are checked, there are differences in the counters. This is because whilst delivering a punch turns the attacker sideways an attack with a kick does not usually do so. Instead of leaving the side of the body open to counter, it opens up the front of the body particularly to a kick. As, therefore, you require a certain amount of space to deliver a kick the stepping back method of defence is particularly appropriate.

While a powerful sweep to the soft underside of the attacker's forearm with the edge of the hand or forearm is very likely to disable the attacker, a similar sweep made against the leg which kicks at you is far less likely to succeed in doing so. The leg is so much more powerful than the arm that although a strong, accurate sweep to the inside of the calf of the leg may be very painful, it is unlikely to have much more effect than that of warding-off the attack. This is important in itself, but it is more important to remember that the wider and farther the leg is swept outwards, the more likely it is to deflect the kick and more it opens up the front of the attacker's body to a counter-attack. It may well be considered better to use a hammer-fist blow when sweeping away a kick than an open-hand cut.

Attack A

Your opponent attacks by kicking forward and upward to your groin with his left foot.

Step I—Deflect the kick away to your right with a downward and outward sweep of your right arm. The fist is first carried up close to the left shoulder and then swept down with fingers extended to make contact with the little finger edge of the hand or forearm or alternatively the little finger edge of the right fist. Sweep away well to the right to separate his legs for your counter-kicks.

As the kick is swept away, step back with the left foot, leaving your weight and balance fully on the right foot. Without any hesitation, kick forward and upward with the left foot, aiming at the opponent's groin which should be fully exposed by your warding-off action. Stretch the toes of the kicking foot forward so that contact is made with the instep. Replace the left foot on the mat, returning to the basic posture.

Step II—Ward-off the opponent's kick with an outward and downward sweep of the right arm, having first taken it up to the left shoulder. The fingers should be extended and contact made with the little finger edge of the hand or forearm or a hammer-fist blow could be used.

At the same time, step back with the left foot, placing your weight equally on both feet. This enables you to use either foot for your counter-attack as you wish or as the opportunity arises. With the left foot, which has been taken back, you kick forward and upward to the groin using the instep to make contact. For the right foot, you must take the hip and foot back to give you room to move and then kick upward and forward at the groin using the toes instead of the instep. This is necessitated because the front of your shin may well be blocked by the underside of the opponent's thigh if an attempt is made to use the instep. Return to basic posture.

Step III—Ward-off the kick with a downward and outward sweep of the right arm using your hand or fist, first taking the hand close to the left shoulder in order to obtain momentum. At the same time, step back with the left foot, immediately transferring all your weight and balance to it.

Without breaking your movement withdraw your right hip and leg and then kick forward and upward with it, aiming your toes at the opponent's groin. Return to the basic posture.

Step IV—Ward-off the attacker's left-footed kick with a powerful downward and outward sweep of the left hand and arm, first having taken the fist up to the area of your right shoulder. Extend the fingers and make contact with the little finger edge of the hand or arm unless you decide to make a hammer-fist attack. Simultaneously, the right leg is taken back, the weight and balance being placed on the left foot, which is not moved.

Without placing the right foot on the ground, kick forward and upward with it to the opponent's groin using the toes to make contact. Resume the basic posture.

Step V—This time the cross-arm defence is used. Take the fists and arms across the body so that they are crossed in front of you. They actually cross about half-way down the forearms. It does not matter which arm is placed on top, if you are going to counter with a leg.

If, however, the counter-attack is to be made with an arm, it must be remembered that only the top arm can be used effectively, as the lower arm may be held too low down to be used effectively for a counter-punch. Block the opponent's left-foot kick with the cross-arm defence, at the same time taking back the left foot, leaving the weight and balance on the right.

At once kick upward and forward to the attacker's groin with the left foot. Use the toes if the kick has been blocked away to the left or directly to the front and the instep if the attack has been blocked to the right. Return to basic posture.

Attack B

The attacker, facing you, aims a forward and upward kick at your groin or stomach with his right foot.

Step I—Deflect the kick away to your left with a downward and outward sweep of your left arm. The fist is first taken close to the right shoulder and then swept down with fingers extended making contact with the little finger edge of the hand or forearm or with the little finger edge of the fist if a hammer-fist blow is used.

Sweep well away to the left so by taking the leg outwards his legs are well separated. As the defensive sweep is made, step back with the right foot, leaving the weight and balance fully on the left foot. Without any break in the movement, at once kick forwards and upwards with the right foot, stretching forward the toes so that your instep is driven upwards into his groin. Replace the right foot on the ground resuming the basic posture.

Step II—Ward-off the kick with an outward and downward sweep of the left arm, first taking the fist from its basic position at the left hip up to the vicinity of the right breast or shoulder. Again, ward outwards very powerfully in order to take the kicking leg well to your left. As you ward-off, step back with the right foot distributing the weight and balance equally between the feet as you replace the right foot on the ground.

At this stage, you can kick upwards and forwards to the groin with the instep of the right foot, or alternatively, take left foot off the ground and withdrawing the left hip and the left leg, kick upwards with it to the opponent's groin.

As the left-foot kick from this position may well be checked by the front of the shin meeting the underside of his right thigh, this kick should be made with the toes and not the instep. Resume the basic posture.

Step III—Ward-off the kick with a downward and outward sweep of the left arm, taking the right foot back as you do so and immediately transferring the weight and balance to that right foot as it is placed on the ground.

Without any break in the movement, withdraw the left hip and leg and kick upward with the toe to the opponent's groin. Finally, return to the basic posture.

Step IV—The right footed kick is warded-off with a downward and outward sweep of the right hand and arm. The fist is taken from the basic position at the right hip to the vicinity of the left shoulder and then with fingers extended sweep across, contact being made with the little finger edge of the hand or forearm. Equally well the hammer fist blow may be used.

At the same time, the left leg is taken back, the weight and balance being retained on the right foot, which does not move. Immediately, the left foot kicks upward and forwards to the opponent's groin, contact being made with your toes. Return to the basic posture.

Step V—For the first time, you use the cross-arm defence. As the opponent kicks with his right foot, your right fist is taken across your body to your left and your left fist across to your right so that your arms cross in front of your body. The cross is made at about the middle of the forearms.

The fists remains lightly clenched to avoid the danger of the fingers being damaged by the kick and the arms are held so that the palms are facing downwards. The arms are held sufficiently in front of you to allow the arms to give to the blow, but still make the defence effective. The kick is now caught or blocked in the V formed by your arms as soon as possible, whilst at the same time, you take your right foot back, leaving your weight and balance on the left foot.

At once, use the free right foot to kick upwards and forwards to the attacker's groin. If the attacker's kick has been warded-away a little to the left the toes should be pointed and the kick delivered with the instep. If the block is made in front of the body or to the right, this may not be possible and the toes should be used. Return to the basic posture.